First published in Belgium and Holland by Clavis Uitgeverij, Hasselt – Amsterdam, 2017
Copyright © 2017, Clavis Uitgeverij

English translation from the Dutch by Clavis Publishing Inc. New York
Copyright © 2017 for the English language edition: Clavis Publishing Inc. New York

Visit us on the web at www.clavisbooks.com

That Looks Good on You! A Visual History of Fashion written and illustrated by Josje van Koppen
Original title: *Dat staat je goed!*
Translated from the Dutch by Clavis Publishing

ISBN 978-1-60537-355-3

This book was printed in July 2017 at Graspo CZ, a.s.,
Pod Šternberkem 324, 76302 Zlín, Czech Republic

First Edition
10 9 8 7 6 5 4 3 2 1

Clavis Publishing supports the First Amendment and celebrates the right to read

THAT LOOKS GOOD ON YOU!

JOSJE VAN KOPPEN

Clavis

NEW YORK

Our clothes make us who we are…

From cave-dwellers to hipsters, from ancient times to the avant-garde, humans have been using clothing for warmth and protection. But we also have been using fashion to express ourselves.

A corseted gown or skinny jeans, flip-flops or platform shoes, a top hat or a knitted cap… clothing is a mirror of our times and a reflection of our unique selves.

Take this visual trip through the history of mankind and fashion. You will see that your own style

always looks good on you!

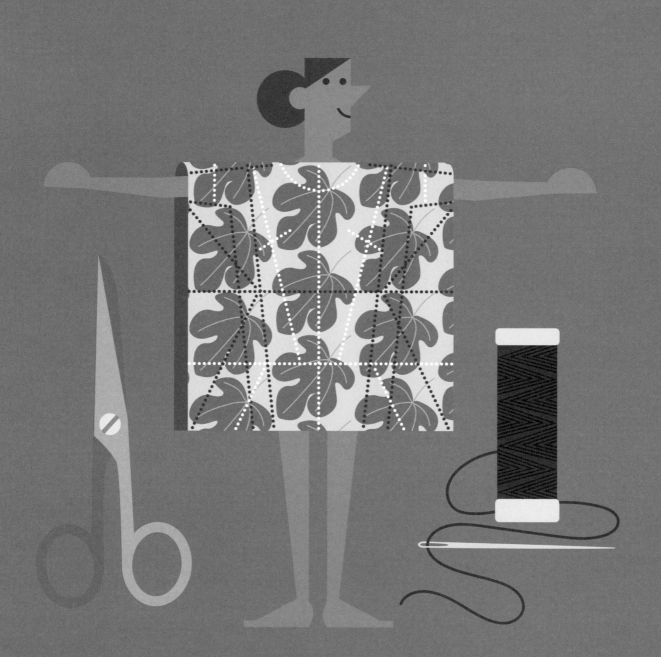

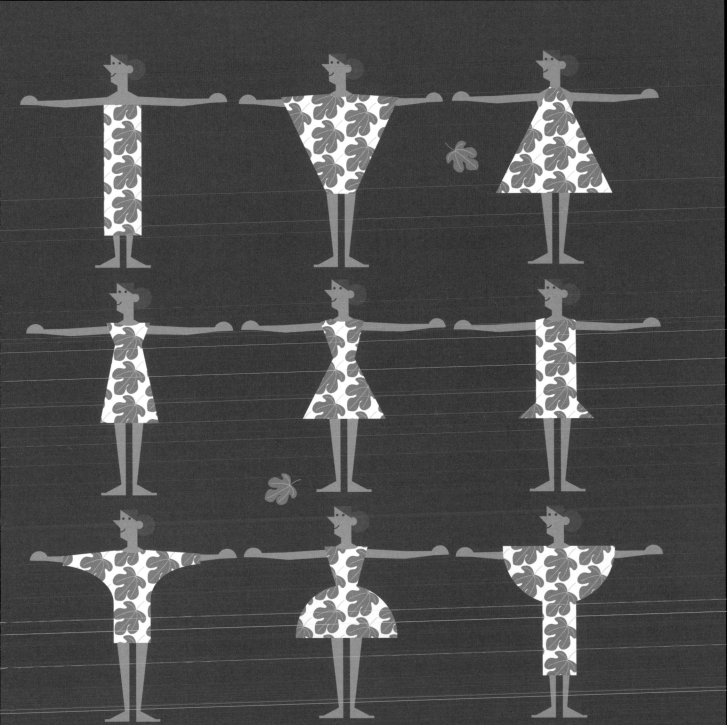

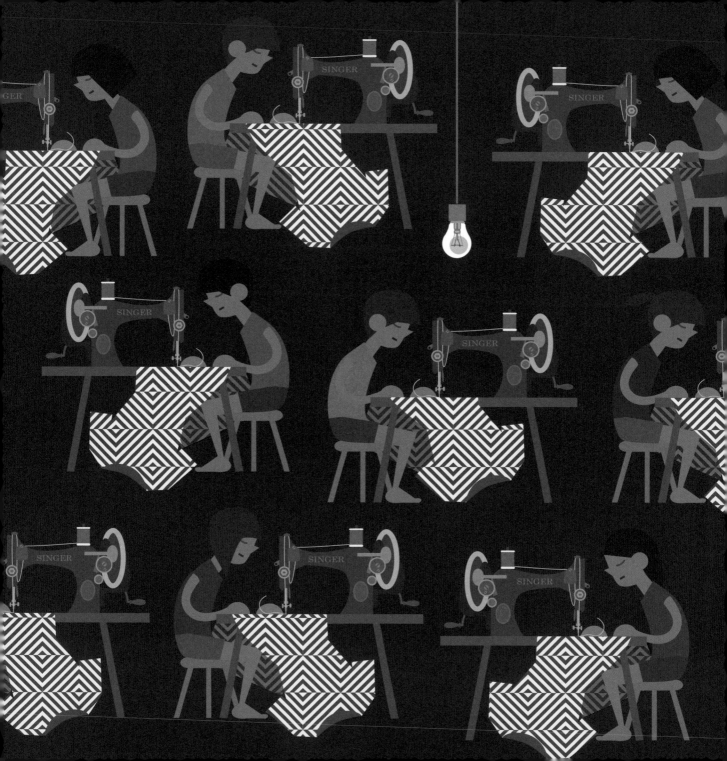

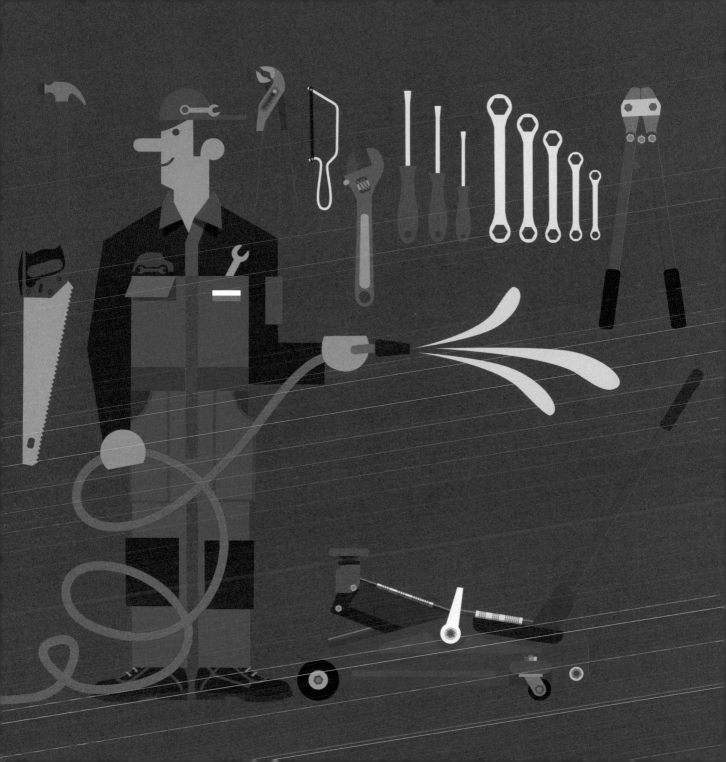

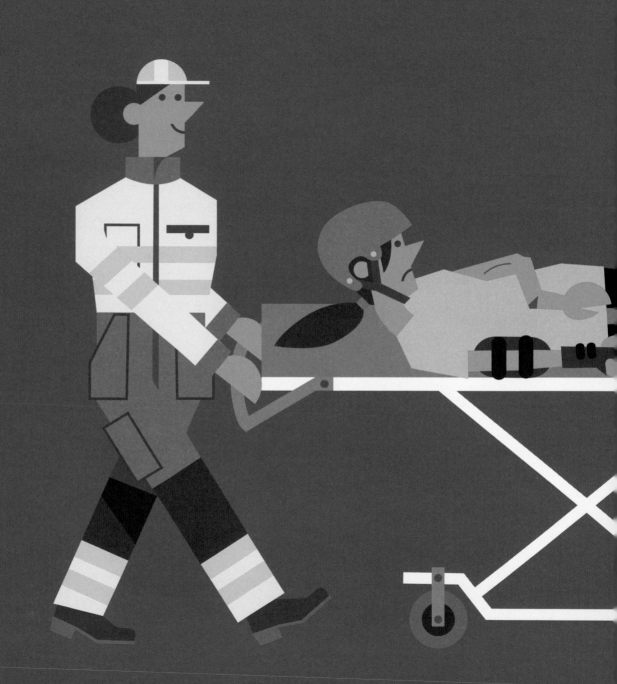

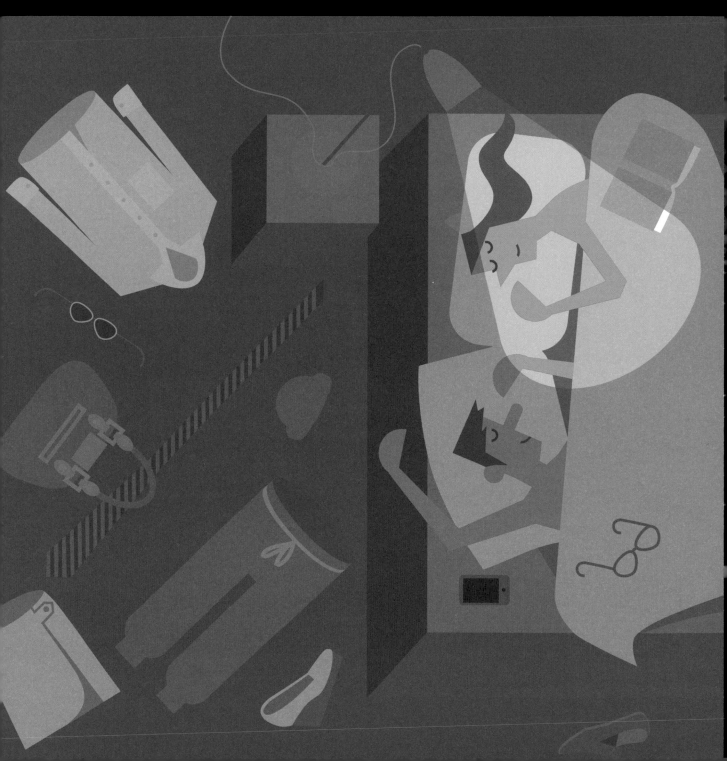

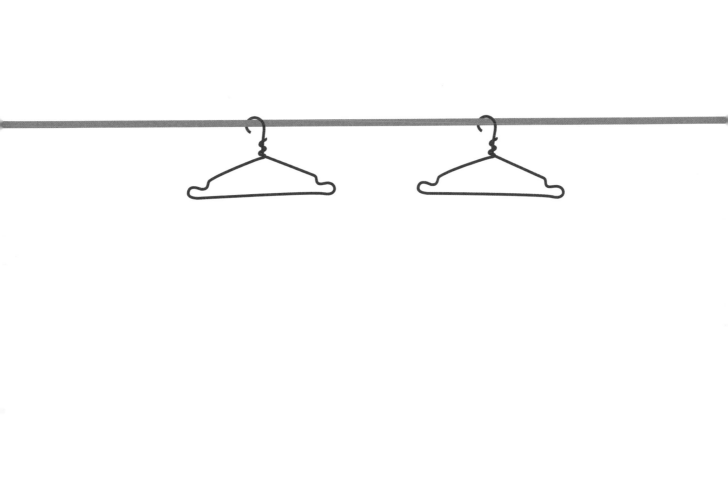

Prehistoric times animal skin/wool

14th century BC Egypt/transparent wool

1st century AD Greece/tunic and cloak

395 Rome/♂ military costume/ ♀ tunic

1350 Middle Ages/ ♂ suit of armor/♀ noble lady

1550 Renaissance/

1778-1790 France/clothes at the court of Louis XVI/♀ coiffure de liberté

1789 French Revolution/clothes as an expression of political ideas

1815 UK/♂ riding clothes/ ♀ redingote, derived from military costume

1800 Empire/♂ dandy/ ♀ gown of thin cloth with empire waist

1830 Biedermeier period

1914 WWI/♂ at the front/ ♀ at work

1920 Roaring 20's/♂ light-colored suit and straw boater/ ♀ corset off, evening gown by Callot Soeurs

1925 ♀ geometric style, manly silhouette

1927 Bauhaus/costumes for the Triadisches Ballet by Oskar Schlemmer

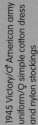

1945 Victory/♂ American army uniform/♀ simple cotton dress and nylon stockings

1947 Post-war period/ New Look by Christian Dior

1950 ♂ trousers and suits with removable suspenders

1953 The American Dream

1955 Rock 'n' roll/musical influences

1967 Flower Power/batik prints, flip-flops, Afghan coat

1967 Pop culture/Jacques Dutronc/Françoise Hardy (dress by Paco Rabanne)

1970 Space Age/Jim Lovell in space suit/♀ dress with go-go boots (André Courrèges)

1970 couture future (Pierre Cardin)

1970 flared trousers, platform sole, floral shirts, man purses, hot pants

1634 Marriage portrait Marten Soolmans/Oopjen Coppit (Rembrandt van Rijn)

1590 Elizabethan England

1640 ♂ Lute-player after Anthony van Dyck/♀ after Wenzel Hollar

1759 Rococo/♂ coat embroidered with wire/♀ mantua (gown) with panniers

1860 American civil war/♂ uniform/♀ crinoline with steel cage

1860 Victorian England/high-necked gown

1900 Belle Epoque ♂ dark suits/♀ bustle-back gown

1913 Art Nouveau/costumes 'Ballet Russes'/evening gown by Paul Poiret

Hepburn (by Hubert de Givenchy)/Brigitte Bardot (Bardot check)

1930 Glamour and decadence/ladies in beach pajamas/Coco Chanel in trousers

1939 Surrealism/Salvador Dalí/Elsa Schiaparelli

1940 WWII/female pilot/lady in a suit

1960 The Beatles/musical influences/jacket by Pierre Cardin & Douglas Millings

1967 Mod/jump suit (André Courrèges)/mini dress (Mary Quant)

1960 ♂ after Marcello Mastroianni (La dolce vita)/♀ cocktail dress (Pierre Balmain)

1965 Mondrian dress (Yves Saint Laurent)

1968 Safari look ♂ & ♀ (Yves Saint Laurent)

1972 jump suits, flared trousers, ViewMaster for the whole family

1975 Punk/safety pins, razor blades, Mohawk haircut

1982 BodyMap (Stevie Stewart & David Holah)

1982 Aerobics (Jane Fonda), legwarmers, fluorescent colors

1985 ♂ Armani suit (Miami Vice)/ ♀ woman's power suit, shoulder pads (Thierry Mugler)

1990 Japan, minimalism/ staircase dress, origami bag (Issey Miyake)

1991 Musical influences/ grunge (Nirvana, among others)

1992 Italy/Gianni Versace

2000 Breton fisher's stripe influences Jean Paul Gaultier/ wedding dress

2000 UK/new value to old traditions (Vivienne Westwood & Malcolm McLaren)

2009 UK/fashion critical of the social structure (Alexander McQueen)

2012-2015 children's fashion after Walter van Beirendonck/ ♂ after Peter Bailey/♀ after Viktor & Rolf

2012 ♂ after Craig Green/♀ after Junya Watanabe (spring 2015)

Child labour/shopaholism

Shopping/vlogging/blogging

Pin-up model/car mechanic

T-shirt shop

workclothes/soldier/judge

workclothes/dishwasher/chef

King Willem-Alexander/Queen Máxima (fashion house Nathan)

uniform/scout

protective clothing

sportswear

trends/onesie

sheltersuit for homeless people (Bas Timmer & Alexander de Groot)

swapping clothes/photography project Switcheroo (Hana Pesut)

descent/faith

party clothes/wedding

dressing up/Thee-act (Mischa van Teeffelen)

traditional costume

butterfly suit after Jeroen van Tuyl (2007)

jeans

WANTED

hipsters/tattoos

after Iris van Herpen (couture 2013)

stress of choosing/dresses

stress of choosing/men

after Walter van Beirendonck (2016)

illustrator Josje van Koppen